AM KEYWORD RESEARCH

A Free Method of Finding Profitable Keywords on Amazon. Increase Sales and Boost Your Rankings Without Paying for Expensive Research Tools.

[Examples & Screenshots Included Inside]

Red Mikhail

Copyright © 2020 2021 by Red Mikhail

The moral right of this author has been asserted.

All rights reserved. No part of this publication may be reproduced, stored in a retrieval system, or transmitted in any form or by any means, without the prior permission in writing from the publisher.

The publisher is not responsible for websites (or their content) that are not owned by the publisher.

TABLE OF CONTENTS

Introduction ... *Page 4*

Chapter 1 – Strategic Keyword Research ... *Page 10*

Chapter 2 – Building Your Master Keyword List for Free ... *Page 18*

Chapter 3 – How to Manage & Input Your Search Terms the Right Way ... *Page 45*

Chapter 4 – How to Optimize Your Listing Keywords by Its Importance ... *Page 51*

Chapter 5 – Amazon Keyword Indexing ... *Page 67*

Chapter 6 - Amazon SEO & Rankings ... *Page 72*

Conclusion ... *Page 77*

Introduction

Welcome to part 3 of the Amazon FBA Business Series.

In the first book of this series, I talked about the process of how a beginner can get started with Amazon FBA. In the second book, I discussed the concept of value skewing and how you can use it to uncover profitable products to sell on Amazon. In this one, I will show you how to find keywords that you can use to increase your sales through Amazon organic rankings.

Keywords are a big part of the whole Amazon ecosystem and they are the bridge between the buyer and the seller. Without proper keyword research and optimization, chaos will ensue because the two parties wouldn't meet. Luckily, Amazon is hell-bent in making sure that this does not happen. With billions of dollars invested in their technology, we can expect that Amazon is doing its best to accurately match the buyer's search intent to the right products that they want or need to buy.

Amazon is a Search Engine

Think of Amazon as an e-commerce search-engine. Amazon wants its visitors to find out what they are looking for. The more accurate the search results are, the better it is for Amazon as a business. This means more sales and more happy customers for them.

The whole system is based on keywords. Keywords that people type on Amazon's search bar. The key difference between Amazon and Google is the buyer's intent behind every search. Amazon searchers are not asking questions, they are looking to buy something already.

According to moz.com, the searches between Amazon and Google ask these fundamental questions:

On one hand, we have Google who asks the question:

"What results most accurately answer the searcher's query?"

Amazon, on the other hand, wants to know:

"What product is the searcher most likely to buy?"

Our job as a seller is to find out what those keywords are. And that's exactly what you're going to learn in this book. You'll discover how to find the best keywords to target for the specific product that you are selling.

1,000 Ft. Overview

Let me walk you through the entire process so you'll have a general idea of how this all works.

In Chapter 1 - Strategic Keyword Research, we'll talk about the mindset that we need to have while doing our keyword research. I'll also discuss why it's so important not to rely on tools alone when it comes to picking your product's keywords. In addition, I'll also give you an overview of where to put your keywords once you already have them.

In Chapter 2 – Building Your Master Keyword List for Free, I'll show you how to create an effective keyword list. You'll also learn some of the best practices to follow when it comes to picking your keywords.

This chapter is going to be extremely practical. You'll learn exactly the digital places to go to whenever you're doing your keyword research. Plus, you'll also get some examples of me doing actual keyword research.
Expect this chapter to be the longest one as this is where you'll learn all the tactics that you need to build your keyword list.

In Chapter 3 – How to Manage & Input Your Search Terms the Right Way, I'll show you how to properly arrange your keywords. I'll also show you how to pick the keywords that you'll put on your title, bullet points, description and the back end of Amazon's metadata for keywords. The key here is not to repeat the keywords too much and plaster it all over your Amazon's listing page. That will serve no purpose and will only be seen by Amazon as over optimization. This is one of the biggest mistakes new Amazon sellers make. They try to rank for big keywords and they end up over-optimizing their Amazon's listing not knowing that there's actually a right blend of keywords and "salability." I'll explain this more later.

In Chapter 4 – How to Optimize Your Listing Keywords by Importance, I'll show you how to properly input your keywords to your title, bullet points, description, features, back-end keywords, and image meta-data.

You can't just randomly input keywords on your listing. Keyword stuffing may increase your chances of getting rank by Amazon in the short-term, but if people are visiting your listing and they end up not buying anyway, Amazon will eventually throw you out of the 1st page.

We want to make sure that you put your keywords in the right place. That means making sure that your listing makes sense to read and isn't just over-optimized with keywords.

We'll go in depth on how you can create the perfect title for your product listing. And we'll also go through some real-world examples and I'll explain why they work in terms of Amazon's ranking and the product listing's ability to sell the product.

In Chapter 5 – Amazon Keyword Indexing, I'll teach you how to check the rankings of your keywords and the possible fixes that you can do to optimize your listing for more traffic.

In Chapter 6 – Amazon SEO & Rankings, I'll show you the exact steps that you can take for your keywords to rank faster on Amazon. We'll discuss tactics like the 2-Step URLS, Super URLs, the Add to Cart Method for maximum Amazon rankings

***

Hopefully, you now have a general idea of how this all works. If not, don't worry about it because I'll discuss all of these steps in detail in each chapter.

For now, I want you to grab a pen & a paper, keep reading and make sure that you take some notes.

What you will be creating (if you follow this guide), will end up as the foundation of your Amazon business. The better you implement the lessons in this book, the more sales you'll have in the future.

Let's do this, shall we?

Chapter 1 – Strategic Keyword Research

In this guide, we are going to focus on free methods and free tools for keyword research.

With so many software tools available now in the market, why are we doing it semi-manually? Why are we focusing on the free methods?

Aside from it being, uhm, FREE – there are 3 main important reasons why we're trying to avoid tools especially in the beginning.

#1 – The Curse of Guru-itis

The #1 reason is because we want to separate ourselves from the competition.

Thousands and thousands of new sellers are starting their own FBA business and most of those people came from some kind of internet marketing guru program.

Trust me, I've taken the $5,000 programs and they are pretty much teaching the same tactics just repackaged as something new.

Imagine 300,000-500,000 individuals following the same old and tired product research and keyword research methods.

These poor individuals end up selling the same thing or end up selling on the same sub-category and they also end up targeting the same keywords.

The reason why these people won't succeed is not because they are terrible at FBA, but because they follow the same method hundreds of thousands of people are also using.
This creates too much competition in the market and 99.9% of them lose their money and quit in the process.

#2 - It Makes You Lazy

Another reason I try not to rely too much on keyword tools is because it makes me lazy.

Instead of mastering the fundamentals, we tend to rely too much on automation and we let the robots think for us. Remember, these tools are only as good as they are programmed to be. These tools don't have any feelings. They do not understand the basic principles of why people type the keywords that they are typing on Amazon's search bar. The software purely relies on data but not on the buying intent of the keyword. This make you miss a lot of potentially profitable keywords that the tools don't include in their scrape.

3 – Tools Do Not Fully Understand Relevancy

Another benefit of doing it manually is you'll be able to find keywords that software tools cannot catch. Unlike humans, these tools doesn't fully comprehend the idea of relevancy. For example, the tools may understand that the keyword *rice cooker* is related to *rice*. But it may not fully comprehend it's relation to other keywords like steamer, stewpot, and sauté.

IS IT GOING TO BE HARDER?

Doing the research manually may seem like stupid at first. It's a little bit harder to do and you'll definitely spend more time compared to just clicking a button on your Amazon keyword research tool.

But the main benefit of this is you're going to find more accurate search terms that your market is actually typing on Amazon's search box.

The result? You'll end up making more money than your competition.

Take the initial hit and work your butt off. The sacrifice you put in today will work wonders for you tomorrow.

SHOULD YOU WORRY ABOUT COMPETITION?

I know what you're thinking. *Free is awesome, but the free method doesn't really show us the number of competition a keyword has. Sure, we can look at the rankings and assume whether it's competitive or not, but the free method doesn't give us the numbers.*

And you are correct for thinking that. Free does not give us the numbers. But the question I want to ask you is this: Is the number of competition really that important?

You would think that it is if you came from the guru school of e-commerce. The truth is, 80% of your income will come from competitive keywords anyway. Sometimes, you'll get lucky and find a non-competitive big market. But most of the time, the product you'll choose will end up super competitive anyway. If you want to make a lot of money on Amazon, then you have to focus on the main keywords. These are keywords that has thousands of searches per month. The other type of keyword is called long-tail. These are keywords with much, much less searches & competition, and they are usually more than 3 keyword terms.

Main Keywords Vs. Long Tail Keywords

Targeting the main keywords is going to be our priority. We want to focus the majority of our time in finding these keywords. Once we have the main ones, we'll start digging deeper in finding the less competitive ones that we can use for additional traffic to our listing.

WHERE TO USE YOUR KEYWORDS:

The keywords you'll eventually choose will have lots of uses for your product. For most newbies, they usually only think about the "backend" or the space where Amazon allows you put your keywords that you want to target. Here are some other areas where you can use your keywords as well.

Title – This is what most people look at first on a listing. Without proper title optimization, you'll be lost with the thousands of products available for sale on Amazon.

Bullet Points – These are the main benefits & features of your product. Putting some keywords in your bullet points also increases your chances of being indexed by Amazon for those keywords.

Description – This part is where you also put the main uses and benefits of your product with much shorter explanation compared to the bullet points.

Backend – This is where you put your keywords in the listing creation part of the process.

Image Metadata – The image's metadata will also have an effect on your keyword rankings.

Amazon PPC – You can use your keywords when you start running Amazon ads.

External PPC – You can also use you keyword list on other ad platforms like YouTube and Google.

We'll talk more about this on Chapter 5 where I'll show you some examples on how you can optimize your keywords for these things.

**

Your Brand as a Keyword

Another awesome thing you can do is to make your brand name part of your keyword strategy. In the beginning, this won't have any effect on your sales. But as your product line gets bigger and bigger, people will start to search for the combination of your brand name and your main keywords.

For example, if you are selling office furniture under the brand name OMEGA, people will eventually start searching for products related to your brand. Keywords like: Omega chairs, Omega desk, and Omega study table to name a few.

***

At this point, you've already chosen your product. (If you haven't done that yet, feel free to check out my book FBA Product Research 101)
Today, you're now looking for a way to increase sales via a smarter strategy for keyword research. This is not the time to fold from the heat. This is the time to implement a smarter strategy than your competition.

Just follow my lead and suspend your disbelief for a minute. Give this strategy a shot and you'll end up much more profitable in the long-run.

A quick note from the author:

I am not against Amazon keyword tools. As you'll see on the next few chapters, they have their own benefits and they can be incredibly useful for Amazon sellers. My point is for you not to rely on them for your keyword research. I want you to differentiate yourself from the masses. I want you to learn the fundamentals of keyword research. By focusing on getting better at this skill, you'll be able to understand why a certain keyword is good and why a certain keyword isn't. Focus on building this skill and you'll be better off than 99% of your competition.

Chapter 2 – Building Your Master Keyword List for Free

So what is a master keyword list anyway?

A keyword list is a combination of all the keywords that you'll target and use for your product. Think of it as the foundation of your building. Without the list, everything will collapse and you'll end up losing the game.

Remember this, your MASTER KEYWORD LIST will consist of keywords that are mostly very competitive by nature. Although we will combine the main keywords and the long-tail keywords, the majority of your traffic will come from the most searched keywords.

The purpose of targeting the very long-tail and less competitive keywords is to use it as hedge against the competition.

The reason we are adding the long-tail keywords is so we can get additional free traffic to our listing.

By its nature, the long-tail keywords are going to be easy to rank for, but they also won't have as much searches as our main keywords.

***

I used to teach this method to a group of intermediate FBA sellers and half the people disagree in my less software-reliant way of keyword research. They're afraid that if we don't look at the numbers, then we won't be able to target the right keywords for the product.

But their reluctance comes from the mindset of a growth-hacker. Most of the time, their focus is on the long-tail keywords. They're afraid of the competition and they want to focus most of their time with the guaranteed less competitive keywords (the long-tail ones).
So are numbers not important? Shouldn't we use the software tools to know how many searches a keyword gets per month?

Well, the numbers are indeed semi-important. But in my experience, they aren't as important as they are hyped to be. They're just there to serve as a guideline. But ultimately, you'll always want to rank for the main competitive keywords because those are the ones that will bring 80% of your sales. You don't need a tool for that because you'll eventually choose the most searched ones for your list.

Why does it matter whether some keyword tool says the competition is high, medium, or low when you'll end up targeting the most searched keywords anyway?!

Rules for Including Keywords on Your Master List.

Before you do your keyword research, make sure that you follow these rules so you don't waste your time. Being efficient and effective is the name of the game. Follow these 3 rules for effective keyword research.

1 - Do Not Include Your Competitors' Brand Name

Unfortunately, tools don't know how to recognize this so you'll end up sorting lots of them anyway. If you do a manual search, you can just avoid putting other company's brand on your list.

At first, it may seem like a good idea to hi-jack a competitor's brand name so you can get a trickle of the traffic they are getting. But this is bad practice because it doesn't serve the purpose of the customers... *which is to find products related to the brand that they searched for.* If they are searching for Unilever products, then it doesn't make sense for Amazon to show non-Unilever items. It doesn't serve the customers and it's not a good look for Amazon if they force other brands down their customer's throat when they're not searching for that brand in the first place.

Now, if you type in a brand name on Amazon, 95% of the products that you will see are under the same seller. But since the system is not perfect, you will still see some other related products that aren't included in the same line of brand that you just searched for.

2 - Do Not Include Any Irrelevant Keywords

Another important thing to avoid is keyword stuffing. Please, please, please. Avoid putting unrelated keywords to your Master Keyword List. It doesn't serve any purpose and it'll just make Amazon's bots confused.

Again, you have to remember what Amazon wants. It wants accurate results so people can buy the product that they are looking for. Adding unrelated keywords may get you some additional traffic but I guarantee you that it will not affect your sales. If anything, people will be pissed at you since you keep coming up on search terms that are completely unrelated to the one they are looking for.

Don't try to be a smartass and go against the grain. I understand the temptation to just put as many keywords as you can whether they are relevant to the product or not. After all, we all just want to put our product out there and make as many sales as we can.

But you have to look at this as a long-term play and trust Amazon's recommended best practices. If you do the right thing now, you'll eventually end up as the winner.

3 - You're Only Allowed 250 Characters

You are only allowed to put up to 250 characters In the back-end optimization part of your Amazon listing. Amazon did this because it wants to avoid keyword stuffing and it wants to create a more accurate set of results for the customers.

That may not seem like a lot especially if you have hundreds of long-tail keywords to include. But don't fret my friend, Amazon allows you to jumble the words and their bot immediately recognizes the possible combination of keywords available at your disposal.

For example:

If you want to rank for keywords like:

[Image 2.1]

Bamboo tooth
Bamboo toothbrush
Bamboo toothpicks
Bamboo toothbrushes soft bristles
Bamboo toothbrushes medium firm
Bamboo toothbrushes case small
Bamboo toothbrushes soft

Then you only need to mention the main keyword *bamboo toothbrush* once. Amazon will automatically recognize and combine it with the other keywords like *toothbrushes, toothpicks, soft, case, bristles, medium*, and *firm*.

In this example, you are not only getting ranked for the 7 keywords that you want, but you're also being naturally optimized for other combinations like:

Soft bristles medium
Soft bristles small
Bamboo toothbrush medium firm
And many other possible combination.

We'll talk more about this once we already completed our list.

STEPS TO BUILDING YOUR KEYWORD LIST.

Here are the steps to building a master keyword list.

Step 0 – Prepare a note or an excel keyword file and name it after your product.

This one is pretty self-explanatory. Just open a note or excel file and copy paste each new keyword that you'll find.

Also, a quick note about duplicates. Don't worry about em', we'll deal with it and arrange them properly on the next chapter. For now, just type in as many keywords as you can gather.

Step 1 – Find Your Competitors

If you're reading this book, then you are most likely already dead set on a product that you want to sell. That means you already have an idea of what type of item you want to create a listing for.

So the first step is to find your competitors' products on Amazon.

I recommend that you gather at least 15 product competitors that are the most relevant and closest to what you're trying to sell.

Let's say that I want to sell a *Bamboo Toothbrush* on Amazon.

The most obvious main keyword is the term "Bamboo Toothbrush" so that's what I'll search for on Amazon.

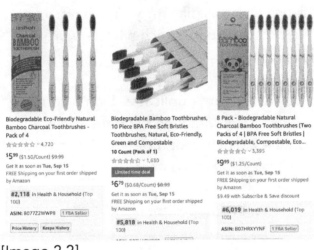

[Image 2.2]

Next, I'll look at the top 10-15 search results and I'll save the product listing links on my notes or excel file.

The more relevant they are to the product that you want to sell, the better.

Step 2 – Grab Your Related Keywords

A Note Before We Gather Our Keywords:

As I've already discussed in the last chapter, I don't want you to worry about the number of competition. Because by default, the keywords that you'll gather later are going to be naturally competitive in nature. Knowing the exact number of searches for all of these keywords can be helpful but also unnecessary for now.

Plus a little fun fact for you. Do you know that most of these "number of searches" that you get from software tools aren't that accurate?

On the latter part of the chapter, I'll show you a free tool that automates the process and shows you the number of approximate volume searches it gets – but for now, knowing the fundamentals is crucial in improving your keyword research skills. Trust me on this :P

So where do we actually get these keywords? I'm glad you asked.

A - Competitor's Product Titles

I always start with the product titles because that's where I'll get my most valuable keywords. The title is where you'll grab most of the main keywords that will serve as your main traffic source. 50% to 70% of your Amazon traffic will come from the keywords that you gather from the title.

Open up the links that you collected and just copy & paste all the titles to your excel file.

Biodegradable Eco-Friendly Natural Bamboo Charcoal Toothbrushes - Pack of 4		
Biodegradable Bamboo Toothbrushes, 10 Piece BPA Free Soft Bristles Toothbrushes, Natura		
8 Pack - Biodegradable Natural Charcoal Bamboo Toothbrushes (Two Packs of 4 | BPA Free		

[Image 2.3]

Make sure NOT to include any of your competitor's brand name in the list.

B - Competitor's Product Bullets

Next, go look at the product bullets of the links you just opened up.

The product bullets are the list that you will find below the title when you open up a product listing.

Get $10 off instantly: Pay $0.00 upon approval for the Amazon Prime Store Card.

- JOIN THE GREEN TEAM- These biodegradable toothbrushes clean our teeth and save our earth from toxic plastics. These firm toothbrushes are BPA- free nylon bristles, with soft bristles and yet crafted in a way that the bristles will never shed away.
- ECO-FRIENDLY TOOTHBRUSHES: Leave the plastic toothbrushes right now! Our Wood Toothbrush BPA FREE nylon bristles is environmentally safe, eco-friendly and acts on the philosophy of Go Green. We ensure that our wooden toothbrushes are made of sustainable and biodegradable material that can easily be recycled. Even the packaging is 100% recyclable.
- NATURAL TEETH WHITENING- Keep the Yellow Teeth Away! These organic toothbrushes will keep your teeth brighter and clean at all times. The activated charcoal toothbrush cleans the sensitive gum walls, removes plaques bad breaths and really keep that smile going.
- GET 8 TOOTHBRUSHES NUMBERED 1-4 - We understand our shoppers want value for their buck and we decided to bring an 8 pack for our customers. And they come with two packages of four. You can use them or spread the Green Movement and make a great gift.

[Image 2.4]

About this item
- [ECO FRIENDLY AND BIODEGRADABLE]: Bamboo toothbrush made from natural sustainable Bamboo farms, our product is 100% Natural! Their quality is as same as your generic plastic brushes but biodegradable.
- [A PACK OF 10 TOOTHBRUSHES]: A pack of ten and each one is individually packaged in cardboard. It is very suitable for family member.
- [EASY TO USE]: No need to dry the bamboo handle after use, Use method the same as the plastic toothbrush.
- [SOFT BPA FREE BRISTLES]: The bristles are made from high-quality nylon which is soft, perfect for getting all the plaque off of your teeth.
- [100% SATISFACTION GUARANTEE]: If there have any problem please contact me, I will provide a perfect solution for you. we support refund within one month and replacement within three months.

[Image 2.5]

If you look at image 2.4 and 2.5, you will find that the main benefits and features are always highlighted in the beginning of each sentence. In addition, they are almost always in capital letter so they are pretty easy to spot.

I want you to copy the keywords and add it to your master keyword list.

In our example, the following keywords I got from my research:

JOIN THE GREEN TEAM
ECO-FRIENDLY TOOTHBRUSHES:
NATURAL TEETH WHITENING
GET 8 TOOTHBRUSHES NUMBERED 1-4
GO GREEN!
SMOOTH & NATURAL BAMBOO HANDLE
100% RECYCLED BIODEGRADABLE PACKAGING

(please refer back to image 2.4 and 2.5 to see these keywords)

Another part of the bullet you can look at is the description after the benefits. Usually, you will find more keywords that makes a lot of sense to add.

In image 2.4, you'll see words like:

Wood Toothbrush BPA FREE nylon bristles

activated charcoal toothbrush
sensitive gum walls
removes plaques bad breaths

These are some long-tail keywords that can add up traffic to our listing without much effort in trying to rank for them.

C – Competitor's Product Information

If you scroll down a little more below the product images, that's where you'll find the product description. Although it may get repetitive at times, you are still likely to find more unique keywords inside the description. You just have to look at ALL the products you gather and really take the time to read them.

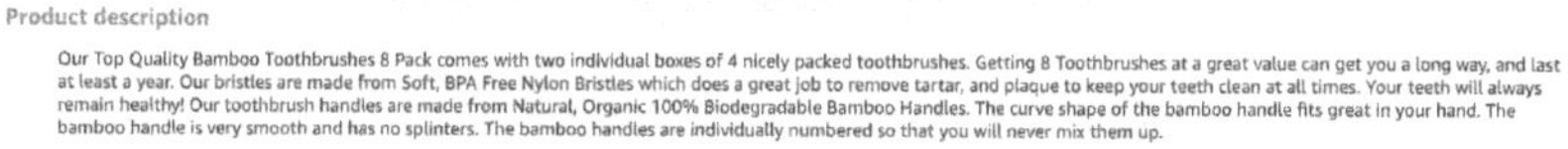

Product description
Our Top Quality Bamboo Toothbrushes 8 Pack comes with two individual boxes of 4 nicely packed toothbrushes. Getting 8 Toothbrushes at a great value can get you a long way, and last at least a year. Our bristles are made from Soft, BPA Free Nylon Bristles which does a great job to remove tartar, and plaque to keep your teeth clean at all times. Your teeth will always remain healthy! Our toothbrush handles are made from Natural, Organic 100% Biodegradable Bamboo Handles. The curve shape of the bamboo handle fits great in your hand. The bamboo handle is very smooth and has no splinters. The bamboo handles are individually numbered so that you will never mix them up.

[Image 2.6]

For example, in this product description from image 2.5, I can see some keywords that I haven't copy pasted in my current master keyword list.

These are keywords like:

Top Quality Bamboo Toothbrushes
nicely packed toothbrushes

Repeat the process and do your research for all the competitor's products that you saved in the first step.

D - Competitor's Product Question and Answer

Another source of additional keywords is the Q & A part of the listing. In here, you'll find the main concerns of the customers and most likely, additional main keywords that will get you a lot of traffic.

Question:	What is the packaging made out of?
Answer:	Hey Stephany!
	The box is made out of cardboard and the individual wrappings are made out of paper.
	Hope that helps and let us know if you have anymore questions!
	Kind Regards,
	-Stacey
	Customer Care Representative see less
	By Avistar SELLER on December 13, 2017
Question:	How soft are the bristles? I prefer using soft or even extra soft
Answer:	Hi, the bristles are medium soft. Feel free to try them out and if they are not to your liking we have a 30 day money back return policy :)
	Kind regards, ... see more
	By Avistar SELLER on June 5, 2018
	˅ See more answers (1)
Question:	Are the bristles also biodegradable?
Answer:	Hey!
	The bristles are not biodegradable however they are recyclable. This was done on purpose because anything other than nylon during our testing posed a danger to the bristles coming undone (which could lead to a mess or even injury). So in order to keep an extremely high quality brush, we decided on making the ... see more
	By Avistar SELLER on December 14, 2017

[Image 2.7]

Make sure that you read the questions and answers and be aware enough of the possible additional keywords you can add to your list. This takes a little bit more time to do but it's well worth the effort since you're going to find keywords that most people just completely ignore.

E - Competitor's Product Reviews

Another type of slightly more intensive research is via the product reviews.

You can add more keywords just by reading as many reviews as you possibly can.

Continuing our Bamboo Toothbrush example, by reading the reviews on dozens of product listings, I found additional keywords that can help me get more traffic on Amazon.

Some of the additional keywords I found are:

Strong Handle Toothbrush
Bristles Tips
Kids Version Bamboo Toothbrush
Combats Bacteria Growth
Cardboard Packaging

A SHORTCUT TRICK:

One trick that you can do to detect the most mentioned keywords is to simply look at the "Read review that mention" section of the Amazon listing.

You'll usually find this above the reviews or below the q & a section. Please see example at image 2.8 and 2.9.

These are the keywords that reviewers are mentioning over and over again. Just make sure that you do this in ALL of the competitor's products that you gather so you'll have more keywords to paste on your Master Keyword List.

For these keywords, try not to include very generic comments like:

Free
Great value
Job done
Feel like
Highly recommended

Try to only put the ones that are highly relevant to what you are selling.

Read reviews that mention

eco friendly	individually wrapped	last as long	toothbrush
amount of plastic	great quality	individual packaging	different colors
highly recommend	bpa free	thrown away	write our names

[Image 2.8]

Read reviews that mention

eco friendly	toothbrush	highly recommend	environmentally friendly
easy to hold	teeth feel	plastic ones	feel like	whole family
getting used	great value	job done	plastic toothbrush

[Image 2.9]

• •

Most of your competitors will skip this because it's labor intensive, but I know that you won't. Why? Because you already know the value of the fundamentals. I've already sold you in the value of manual research first before utilizing the software tools available in the market.

Look, I know that this is additional work but it's something that I believe is worth the effort. You'll leap ahead your competition because you're ready to do the things that they aren't willing to do.

Step 3 – Adding More Keywords

So you've gathered your keywords and by now, you've collected a pretty solid list of potentially profitable terms to use.

Now it's time to take it up a notch and go further than your competition.

I recommend adding 3 more research methods to your disposal so you can get that extra oomph.

Also, doing these 3 keyword methods may help you find more unique keywords that you didn't find in your initial research.

Sure, you can skip this if you want to, but why would you? Do you hate money or something? I'm just here to help you and give you more options. So hurray for options!

Here are some more additional free keyword research methods that you can use.

A - Amazon Keyword Search Bar

Quite frankly, the easiest way to target keywords that people are already searching for.

It's free, it's simple, and best of all – it's effective.

By doing an Amazon Keyword Search using the search bar, you are almost guaranteed to find high volume/regularly searched keywords inside Amazon.

Let's continue with our example of Bamboo Toothbrush.

Just go to Amazon's search bar, pick the category of the product (or just choose ALL DEPARTMENTS) and type in your main keyword.

In our case, I would type in the word BAMBOO TOOTHBRUSH and then wait for Amazon to show the dropdown suggestions.

Please see image 2.10 for the visuals.

[Image 2.10]

Some of the keywords you'll find are probably already in your list. However, sometimes, you do get to find unique keywords that you haven't thought of.

You can also search for anything related to your product.

So if yours is a Bamboo Toothbrush, then just search for the word "Bamboo" or "Toothbrush" separately.

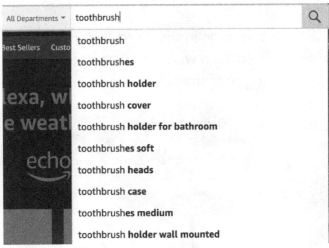

[Image 2.11]

After searching for your keywords, frankly, you just have to use your common sense to know if you should put the new keywords you just found.

Ask yourself, *does it make sense to add that keyword?*

For example, in image 2.11, I search for the word "toothbrush" and Amazon gave me additional keywords like "holder", "cover", "Bathroom", "holder wall mounted" and "case"…

These are all keywords that are very related to what I'm trying to sell so I can add them to my master list.

However, if you look at image 2.12, when I search for the word "Bamboo", all I found are keywords like pillow, cutting board, streamer, skewers, and paper towels.

Uhm, yeah – so there's absolutely no relevance to what we're trying to sell so there's no point in including those terms to the master list.

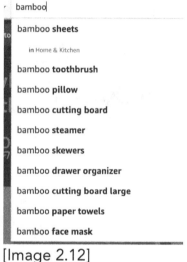

[Image 2.12]

I do advice that you search for as many keywords as you can and find as many relevant once that you can put in the list.

B - Using Google Keyword Planner for More Ideas

Admittedly, using Google Keyword Planner's as a research tool won't give us as much traffic as we do targeting Amazon based searched terms.

However, it's still a great tool to add more potential keywords that we might have missed in our prior research.

To use Google's Keyword Planner, log-in to your Gmail account and go to the following link:

https://ads.google.com/aw/keywordplanner/home

Then use the feature "Discover New Keywords."

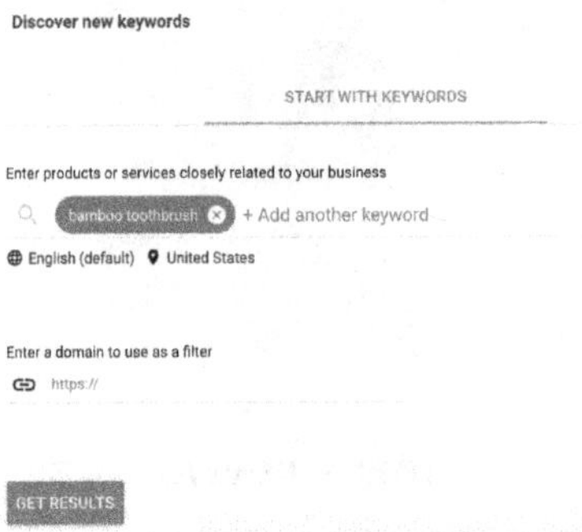

[Image 2.13]

Target "United States" as the country and English as the default language. Input your search term and click the GET RESULTS button.

Download the results and add them to your master list.

Important Note: Make sure that you remove any results with other companies' brands.

Another very smart thing that you can do is to copy and paste your competitors Amazon listing via the START WITH A WEBSITE search query.

[Image 2.14]

Use English as default language, choose United States as the country and then click the "Use only this page" button, and then click GET RESULTS.

Download the results and add the keywords to your master list.

Repeat this process over and over again by copying and pasting your Amazon competitor's listing link on the GKP's START WITH A WEBSITE search bar.

You'll eventually find duplicates from your Amazon research but don't worry about it. We'll sort all of that out in the next chapter.

C - Amazon AHREFS – Free or Cheap Method

By now, you should already have a pretty intensive list. But feel free to add this one more method of keyword research to your arsenal.

From time to time, I will also use a keyword software called Amazon AHREFS.

You can get a limited number of keywords by using the free feature or you can pay for $7 for 7 days and just gather as many keywords as you can.

The choice is totally up to you.

You can go to this link to use the ahrefs tool:

https://ahrefs.com/amazon-keyword-tool

Then just search for your keyword and look for additional terms you can add to your list.

[Image 2.15]

Ahref shows the volume of the search terms so that's an added feature that can help you in analyzing the competition.

Keyword	Volume
bamboo toothbrush	41K
bamboo toothbrush holder	1.0K
bamboo toothbrush soft bristle	900
bamboo toothbrush kids	500
brush with bamboo toothbrush	500
bamboo toothbrush medium bristles	450
bamboo toothbrush case	250
soft bamboo toothbrush	200
bamboo toothbrush medium	200
bamboo toothbrush soft	200
charcoal bamboo toothbrush	200
kids bamboo toothbrush	200
bamboo toothbrush charcoal	150
bamboo toothbrush travel case	100
mable bamboo toothbrush	80
mothers vault bamboo toothbrush	80

[Image 2.16]

You can copy-paste the terms to your master list or download them in excel if you have the paid version.

Again, remove the keywords with brand names in them. You don't want to rank for your competitors keywords as it will make Amazon's search results confusing.

Why Did We Use This Keyword Tool Last?

Did we just wasted our time doing it manually? Can't we just start with the keyword tool instead? Sure you can, but you'll miss important relevant keywords that these kind of tools tend to miss.

The purpose of this book is not to show you how to rely on keyword tools. The purpose of this book is to give you the fundamentals of research so you'll have an advantage over the competition whether you use keyword research tools or not.

▪▪

Hopefully, I was able to give you an in-depth look on how to do Amazon keyword research. I must admit. It's not as sexy as *clicking a few buttons and just looking at the results, and then boom! You're done.* But I hope that I was able to impart the basics and the key steps that you need to do to maximize your keyword research.

Now that you completed your master keyword list, it's time to arrange them properly so we can maximize its effectiveness.

Chapter 3 – How to Manage Your Search Terms the Right Way

Now that you have completed your master keyword list, the next step is to remove the duplicates and find the most searched keyword terms to save and later input on the backend keywords tab of our Amazon listing.

You should already have hundreds if not thousands in the list.

To arrange our keywords, we're gonna need a tool called Helium10.

Don't worry, like most of the tools we use in this book – it's 100% free, but only for 30 days. The good news is we don't need a credit card to sign-up for a free trial.

You can sign up through this website:

http://www.helium10.com

Helium is an Amazon research tool for Product Research, Keyword Research, Operation, Listing Optimization, Marketing and Analytics.

As you can see, it's pretty much an all in one tool for Amazon sellers.

However, we're only going to focus on one key feature which is called Frankenstein. You'll also have very limited access to the other features if you're on a 30 day trial.

Once you got your account, just simply go to the Listing Optimization tab and click on Frankenstein.

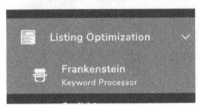

[Image 3.1]

Then copy and paste all your keywords in the "Original Keywords" section.

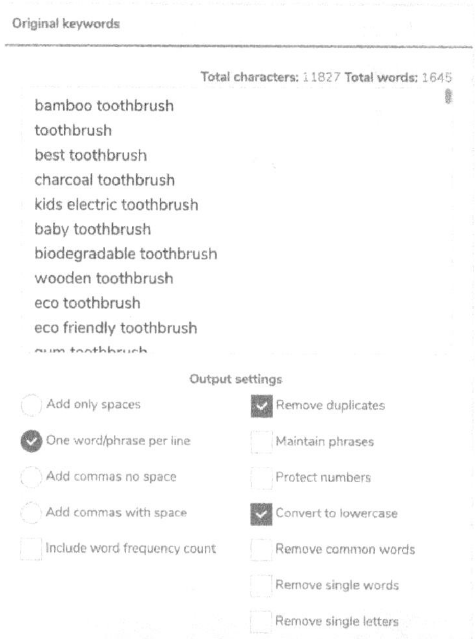

[Image 3.2]

Then follow this output setting:

1 – One word/phrase per line
2 – Remove duplicates
3 – Convert to lower case

Then on the right side of the original keyword section, click on frequency.

When you look at your keywords, you will see the most frequent keywords that are searched over and over again.

Most likely, the first 5-10 results are your main keywords. They are the keywords where more than 40% of your traffic will come from if you're on the first page of Amazon for those keywords.

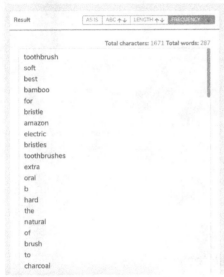

[Image 3.3]

The next step is to browse your list and look for non-relevant keywords that you can remove.

If you already did your manual research and actually removed your competitors brand name and other non-related keywords, then you are set and you don't have to change anything in the list. Or at the very least, you only have to remove a few keywords that were able to snuck in there.

If you got a little lazy in that regard, then now is the time to remove those brand names and non-relevant keywords.

The only advice I can give you here is to use your common sense.

For example. In my own keyword list I found that there are words like:

bigelow
month
music
choosing
swissco

These are obviously not related to bamboo toothbrush, so I'll just manually remove them.

Once you're done with that step, just click the "Add Only Spaces" in the output settings to re-arrange your keywords.

(Please see image 3.4 for an example)

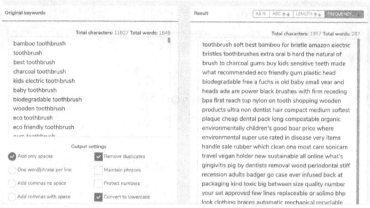

[Image 3.4]

The final step is to click save which lets you download the list as a text file.

These are the keywords that you'll paste later on the backend section of your listing. Congratulations, the first part of your keyword optimization is done.

●●

The next step in the process is to optimize our listing for the keywords that we want to rank for. We don't want to rely on Amazon's backend keywords alone. We also have to put our keywords in our listing.

So how do we actually do that?

Chapter 4 – How to Optimize Your Listing Keywords by Importance

What's the point of research if you won't be able to use your keywords properly anyway? In this chapter, I'm going to show you how to properly optimize your keywords for maximum effectivity. If you skip this step, then you won't be able to rank and you'll lose potentially thousands of dollars in sales.

There are a lot of factors that may affect the rankings for your search terms, things like title, backend keywords, and description to name a few.

Here are Some Rules to Remember Before You Start Your Listing Optimization:

1 - Do Not to Repeat the Keywords

Amazon is smart. It knows when you're repeating keywords and Amazon will just recognize this as one search term. That means putting your main keyword over and over again (especially in the backend section) doesn't really do anything for you. In fact, it just hurts you because more repeated keywords means less space for more unique keywords to put in there instead.

So repeating keywords is useless and is a big waste of space.

2 - Don't Sacrifice Readability for Keyword Stuffing

It's inevitable that you'll use some keywords over and over again. Sometimes, it just makes more sense to mention some certain keywords. For example, if your main keyword is "Bamboo Toothbrush", then there's a good chance that you'll mention that keyword on your title, description, and backend keywords. That's perfectly fine.

What's not okay is to just randomly put them all over your listing for the sake of keyword rankings.

You can't be putting that keyword wherever you like. The title, description, features, and bullet points still has to be readable.

The reader must not be distracted by our keyword placement and it has to look natural. I see a lot of over-optimized product listings out there and they are horrible to read.

For example, I found this bamboo toothbrush listing with the title:

ecofworld USDA Certified Natural Bamboo Toothbrushes with Round Handle Biodegradable Eco-Friendly Vegan - Compostable Organic Reusable Wooden Brush | Medium Firm Bristle | Adult Multi-Color (5 Pack)

It's a terribly obvious attempt to rank for as many keywords as he can, but damn, it's a long title and the words doesn't really flow when you read it.

3 - Do Not Use Other Company's Brand Names

I already mentioned this quite a few times but I'm saying it again. Do not use other company's brand names and use your own brand instead.

You don't want to rank for your competitor's brand names. It's disingenuous and it doesn't serve the customer's best intention. You have to remember what I told you in the first chapter.

"Amazon wants its visitors to find out what they are looking for. The more accurate the search results are, the better it is for Amazon as a business. This means more sales and more happy customers for them."

The more you abide by Amazon's rules, the more you are likely to get sales. Don't look for shortcut or any blackhat tactics. Just focus on what's good for the customers. If you do this, I guarantee you that

Amazon will reward you with higher rankings and more exposure in their product recommended section below your competitors listing.

The point is you have to trust Amazon that it will do you right. But first, you have to play the game by their rules. At the end of the day, Amazon's main mission is not just profits, but this:

"We strive to offer our customers the lowest possible prices, the best available selection, and the utmost convenience."

Can you support Amazon in doing that mission?

If yes, then you will also prosper.

If you want to learn more about how Amazon as a company thinks and make decisions, I recommend reading Jeff Bezos' letters to shareholders.

You can download them here:

https://drive.google.com/file/d/1e_5uxXpfFD0Yic6xnCcxLAmmhP_FGv_d/view

or this link: shorturl.at/noquA

Now let's move on to optimizing your keywords for maximum effectiveness.

Your Listing By Importance:

I have to be honest with you. Nobody really knows what the exact Amazon algorithm is and how they approach this as far as keyword ranking goes. But what I can give you is an educated guess based on my own experience and the experience of countless FBA sellers I have worked with over the last decade.

Based on my experience, this is the ranking of the listing part by its importance:

#1 is the Title
#2 is the Backend Keywords
#3 is the Bullet Points
#4 is the Description
#5 is the Image Metadata

1 - Creating a Traffic Grabbing Title Using Your Keyword List

Your title is the most important text in your listing so you should spend a lot of time trying to come up with the most effective one you can think of.

Title Requirements

Before you create your title, I recommend that you familiarize yourself with the following guidelines.

A – Product Title Must Not Exceed 200 Characters Including Spaces.

Amazon only allows up to 200 characters for the title. So you have a very limited amount of space. In addition, super long titles tend to get skipped at especially if they are not optimized for readability.

B – Do Not Use Forbidden Promotional Words

Forget about using words like *free*, *sales*, or *limited promo*. Amazon hates these type of words as it distorts their search results.

C - Do Not Put the Price of the Product

Product price always changes based on Amazon's algorithm so don't put the price on the title.

D – Do Not Use Subjective Terms

Avoid using subjective terms like *best, fastest, sure-ball*, and *guaranteed* on the title as it doesn't present the product in a factual way.

E – Do Not Use Any Special Characters

Avoid using any special characters like TM, @, # or !.

F – Do Not Repeat Any Keywords

....

A Simple Formula for Creating An Effective Title

Here's the formula I follow whenever I'm creating a title.

Brand Name + Primary Keywords + Main Features

1 – Start with your brand name. Always put your brand name in the beginning of your listing. This creates separation from the crowd and it lets you build familiarity which allows you to expand with more products in the future.

2 – Choose the top 2-3 terms to put on your title as primary keywords. Make sure that they are relevant.

3 – Then add the most important features your customers need to know. Also, if you read customer reviews from other listings, I guarantee you that you'll know exactly what to put on here.

Here's an example of how I would create a listing title.

Let's continue with our product, bamboo toothbrush.

Step 0 – Gather the text file that you made from chapter 3.

Step 1 - Brand Name.

Ortho-Max

Step 2 - Primary Keywords

I found that the top 3 most repeated keywords according to my research are:

Biodegradable - Bamboo - Toothbrush

Step 3 - Main Features

To find out what the features are, look at your keyword list and copy not only the most repeated search terms but also the biggest features that people are looking for based on your research. Also, make sure that they accurately depict your product. If your product is not vegan, then don't put the keyword *vegan* just because it's in your list.

For my example, my feature would be the following: *Eco Friendly, Soft Nylon Bristles, Organic, Smooth Handle, and 100% Recyclable.*

If I add all of these, my title would something like:

Ortho-Max | Biodegradable Bamboo Toothbrush | Eco Friendly, Soft Nylon Bristles, Organic Material, Smooth Handle, 100% Recyclable.

Quick tip: Make sure that you use a vertical bar to separate the 3 parts.

2 - Backend Keywords

This is actually pretty simple since you've already done the work in chapter 3. You just need to copy and paste your collected text file in the search terms section as you upload your listing. Just make sure you remove your competitors' brand names and only put the relevant keywords there.

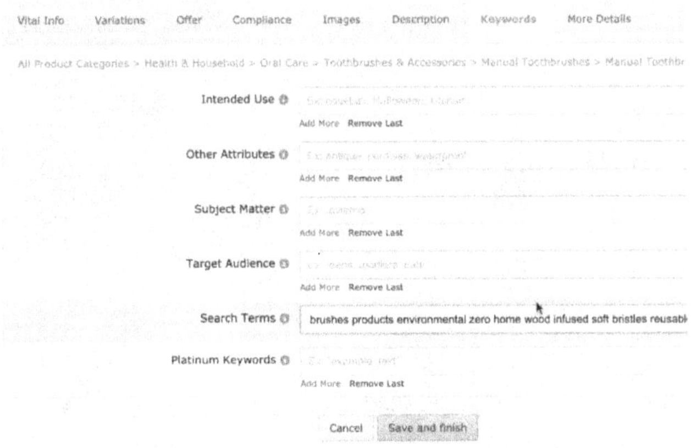

[Image 4.1]

3 - Bullet Points

Your bullet points has 2 main purpose.

#1 – Keyword Relevance

It should let the Amazon bots know that your product is related to whatever product line you're trying to sell. This is pretty simple since you already have a keyword list. All you have to do is arrange them in a readable manner.

#2 – To Sell Your Product

Another purpose of the bullet points is to sell your product. You have to give them a compelling enough reason why they should choose your products over the hundreds if not thousands of the other ones out there.

Bullet Point Requirements:

1 – Do not use symbols, periods, hyphens and question marks.

2 – Separate phrases with semi colon instead of a dash.

3 – Capitalize the first phrase (or the main feature). I'll show you how to apply this in the example section.

4 – Use the actual number instead of the spelling of the number. This gathers more attention and also saves you some characters available for your bullet point.

FORMULA FOR MAXIMUM SALES

I just pretty much follow the same formula over and over again for all of my listings.

Here it is:

Line #1 - Feature + Benefits

I give them the biggest and most important feature that they are looking for and I explain how this affects them.

Line #2 - Feature + Benefits

I give them the 2nd biggest feature that they are looking for and I explain how this affects them.

Line #3 – Differentiate

I try to differentiate my product through a specific feature or benefit.

Line #4 - Twist the Knife + Solve the Problem

I give them a big problem and then I explain to them how my product solves this problem.

Line #5 - Guarantees

I give them some sort of guarantee that the product works or else they can send it back to me and get a 100% refund.

Here's a great example that you can study:

- ★ GO GREEN! – Why fill up landfills with plastic when you don't have to? Help the environment, and feel better about your mark on this world with Bamboo Toothbrush! It's the ecological way to not only keep your mouth fresh for just as long as a normal toothbrush, but help the environment at the same time!
- ★ A PACK OF 4 TOOTHBRUSHES – will last one person a full year. Buy a pack of 4 toothbrushes for each person in your household.
- ★ SMOOTH & NATURAL BAMBOO HANDLE – will never splinter and is water resistant. Stronger and harder than wood, Bamboo is also more durable and healthier than any plastic. No need to dry the handle after use, just rinse your toothbrush and put back into its holder, just like you would with any other old plastic toothbrush
- ★100% RECYCLED BIODEGRADABLE PACKAGING – even the packaging is made in craft paper,no worry about it polluting the environment when you throw it away
- ★ GUARANTEED – We love this toothbrush, and we're sure you will to. However, if for any reason you don't, no worries! Just send it back our way for a full refund of the purchase price. It's natural quality with an unbeatable guarantee. Why keep looking when you've found your solution right here!

[Image 4.2]

If you're listening to the audio version, you can refer to image 4.2 on the accompanying pdf file to look at the example.

Some notes about the example:

Note #1 – Make sure that you use all capital letter for the first line of the bullet point.

Note #2 – The example shows a star symbol before the main keyword, avoid doing that as it is quite unnecessary.

Note #3 – Do the following before you write your benefits.

2 quick tips to know what to put on your bullet points.

Tip #1 - Read the negative reviews and let them know that your product solve these problems.

Tip #2 - Look at the most reviewed listings and copy what they are doing. (Try to rephrase and add your own unique benefits so you won't get accused of being a copycat)

4 – Description

I always try to make my description as short and as concise as possible. The goal of your description is not to sell the product but to give them a brief overview of what they are getting.

Here's a simple formula that I like to follow:

Overview:

First, I give them a quick-run down of the features of my product. A quick-trick that you can do is to grab all the first line of your bullet points and use them as your overview. 1-2 sentences is enough for this part.

Dimension/Specs

The next part is to mention the dimension and specs of your product. 1-2 lines is more than adequate.

Warranty or Guarantee

Just repeat what you said in the guarantee part of your bullet point but make it shorter.

5 - Image Metadata

This is another optimization that literally takes 30 seconds to do. Amazon takes into account the metadata inside your product images. So, all you have to do is change the file name of your files to your main keywords. The more images you have, the more keywords you can use.

Please see Image 4.3 and Image 4.3 for an example.

[Image 4.3]

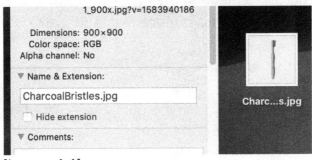

[Image 4.4]

Chapter 5 – Amazon Keyword Indexing

Once you already have a listing, we want to make sure that the keywords we are targeting for are getting indexed by Amazon. If they're not getting indexed, then you're not gonna get any free traffic for those keywords.

Being indexed for your keywords also reduce our reliance to Pay Per Click marketing and allows us to increase market share.

So, how long does it take for us to get indexed?

Usually, it takes less than 24 hours after our listing goes live.

But that doesn't take into account where you are on Amazon's search results. Being indexed doesn't mean you're already on page 1. Being indexed only means you already appear on the search results for that specific keyword, between page 1 or page 500.

So, how do we get indexed?

There are 3 main factors that affects your listing's ability to get indexed for some keywords. Those factors are:

- **Your Title**

    You must put the keywords you want to rank for on your title.

- **The Bullets**

    You must include your main keywords in the bullets section of your listing.

- **Back End Search Terms**

    You must input relevant keywords to your backend search terms.

    The good news is, at this point, you don't really have to do anything anymore. I already taught you how to properly optimize your listing.

    Now it's time to see if you are getting indexed by Amazon. Again, wait for at least 24-48 hours before you do this.

HOW TO KNOW IF YOU ARE GETTING INDEXED BY AMAZON

First, go to Amazon and search for your keyword + your product's ASIN.

You can find your ASIN in your listing.

Please see image 5.1 for an example.

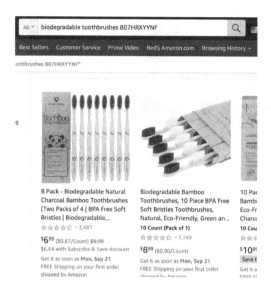

[Image 5.1]

If your product listing appears on the search results, then that means you are being indexed by Amazon for that keyword.

If you didn't appear in the search results, then you are not getting indexed for that search term.

Here's an exaggerated example.

Please see image 5.2 for the visual.

When I searched for "monkey stuff toy + the ASIN", the product listing for the bamboo toothbrush product didn't appear on the search results.

This means that this product is not getting indexed for the keyword "monkey stuff toy"

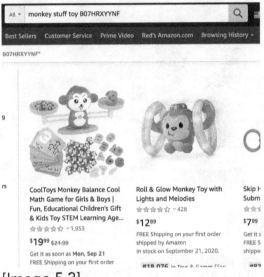

[Image 5.2]

Now, what if I search for a relevant but generic keyword like "toothbrush" instead of "Bamboo Toothbrush"

Guess what the search results will be like?

[Image 5.3]

With this keyword term, I still found the product listing in the search results.

This means that this product is also getting indexed for the keyword "toothbrush."

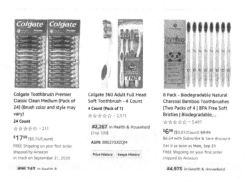

[Image 5.4]

And that's how easy it is to know if you're getting indexed or not.

If you want to pay for automated tools, apps or chrome extensions, you can easily find those just by searching for "Amazon Keyword Ranking or Amazon Index Checker" on Google or the Chrome Web Store.

Chapter 6 – Amazon SEO & Rankings

So how do we increase our chances of ranking on the first page of Amazon for our main keywords? How can we actively help Amazon bots to decide what's best for the customers?

Note: Amazon doesn't allow any type of search ranking manipulation, they specifically said *"Activities that could be perceived as attempting to manipulate Amazon's search results or sales rankings"* is forbidden.

So what I'm going to show you in this chapter is a little bit on the gray area. I am not encouraging that you rely on them for rankings. At the end of the day, your product quality and the value you provide through your product is still the most important part of your brand's success. Proceed with caution and make sure that you read Amazon's terms & conditions before you do any type of AMAZON SEO.

With that said, here are 3 main strategies that you can apply to increase your chances of being on Amazon's page one.

1 – Super URL

A Super URL is basically a link that goes directly to your product listing… but with a twist.

A normal product link would look like this:

https://www.amazon.com/dp/B07FZ8S74R/

A Super URL adds a keyword in the end or middle of the link. This "tricks" Amazon into thinking that the buyer organically searched that specific keyword to find your product. This helps in ranking your product listing for that keyword.

Here's how to create a Super URL.

Step 1 – Find your ASIN

Find & save your product's ASIN.

Step 2 – Add your main keyword in the middle of the link amazon.com and your ASIN. Make sure that you separate 2 terms by using a dash.

Here's what a SUPER URL would look like:

https://www.amazon.com/**biodegradable-toohbrush**/dp/B077Z2WWP8

In this specific example, you just created a super url for the keyword "biodegradable toothbrush". Every sale that will come from that link will be credited to that keyword and it will help you rank organically for that term as well.

The more people buy using your Super URL, the higher your rank will be on the organic search. Most people use Pay Per Click platforms like FB Ads and Google AdWords to advertise their product using a Super URL.

2 – The 2-Step URL

While a Super URL goes directly to a product page, a 2-step URL goes to a search result instead.

Amazon is cracking on people who try to manipulate results and a lot of scammers have discovered the power of Super URLs. They still work but not as much as before.

A 2-step url mimics a more natural approach to Amazon SEO.

Instead of making the customers directly go to the listing page, we try to mimic a natural search instead.

Here's how to create your 2-Step URL.

Step 1 – Find your product's ASIN.

Step 2 – Go to the free sellerapp via this link:

www.sellerapp.com/amazon-super-urls.html

Copy and paste your main keyword and the ASIN to their respective tabs.
Click generate and save your new 2-step url.

This 2-step url link will go to a search result that only shows your product.

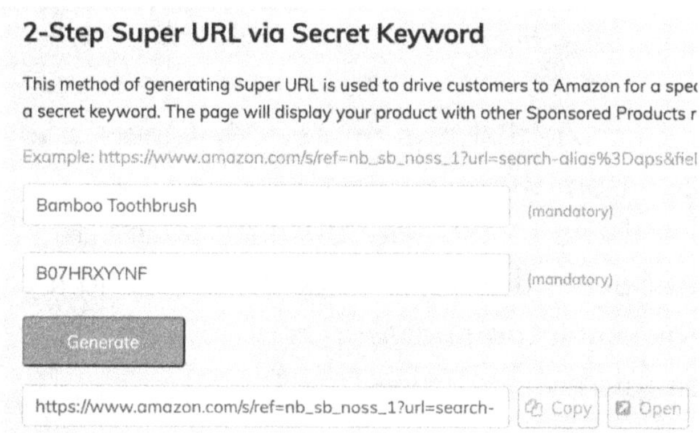

[Image 6.1]

The same with a Super URL, the more people buy using your 2-Step URL, the higher your rank will be on the organic search. Try to use as many diverse traffic source if you can so you'll have a more natural link pattern.

These traffic sources may include: Your Blog, Facebook Ads, Instagram Ads, YouTube Videos, Tweets, and Organic Facebook Shares.

3 - Add to Cart Method

This isn't as powerful as making someone buy your product via a super URL, but it's free and you only need a handful of friends to do this.

To apply the add to cart method, you just have to ask friends and family that lives outside your zip code to add to cart your product. Give them either your super url or your 2-step url for this method.

This works because it shows Amazon that there's an intent to buy from those who searched for your keywords and add to cart your product. It isn't as effective as buying the product itself but adding it to cart does help in letting Amazon know that this is a product people are searching for.

Final Note: Please proceed with caution if you decided to do any of the 3 methods I showed you. Amazon's terms isn't really specific so it's very hard to know what's allowed and what isn't. Make sure that you read their *Terms & Conditions* for more updated information about this.

Conclusion

Amazon Keyword Research is a crucial part of making money on Amazon. It's something that you have to learn yourself before you let your virtual assistant or anyone else do it for you.

Let me give you a brief summary of the entire process.

Step 1 – Understand the fundamentals behind good keyword research. The more solid your foundation is, the better your results will be.

Step 2 – Build your master keyword list that you can use for your title, bullets, description and backend search terms.

Step 3 – Arrange and manage your search terms the right way.

Step 4 – Optimize your listing for maximum effectiveness by putting the keywords on the right place.

Step 5 – Check if your keywords are getting indexed by Amazon.

Step 6 – Rank your keywords faster by applying the top 3 Amazon SEO strategies.

Hopefully, I was able to give you everything you need to get started.

I know that there's probably dozens of ways to do this and I am grateful that you gave this little book a chance.

What I love about this method of research is it's free and any beginner can use it. The little guy will now have to same opportunity as the big guys even if he or she didn't have the budget for it.

I hope that my keyword research process served you well.

Let's Talk About Tools One More Time

Before we part ways, I just want to clarify once again that I am not against automation tools. I think they are great and they are awesome because it makes research easier for all of us. What I am against is overreliance on those tools. I don't want you to forget about the fundamentals of research. We all use calculators nowadays but it's still crucial to know the multiplication table by memory. What I taught you in this book are the fundamentals. The stuff that won't change anytime soon. The knowledge that you can use 2, 5 or even 10 years from now.

Thank you for taking the time to read this short book and I wish you all the best in your Amazon business.

Good luck,

Red

Review Request

As you might already know, reviews are the lifeblood of every author out there. If you found some value in this one, allow me to humbly ask for a review on Amazon as it does help in spreading my message.

Thank you so much, and good luck with your e-commerce business.

Fulfillment by Amazon for Beginners

If you like to learn a simple and step by step way of getting started with Amazon FBA, I recommend that you check out my other book **AMAZON FBA Step by Step** and **FBA Product Research 101**. These are also available as audiobooks.

Just like this one, these 2 have a very simple language and conversational tone to it. If you found this book valuable, then you will like those 2 books as well.

OTHER BOOKS

I also have other books about making money online through different ways:

Amazon's Associate Program

One Hour Dropshipping System

Amazon Product Listing Formula

AMAZON FBA FUTURE UPDATES:

We're just scratching the surface. In the next 12 months, I'm going to launch a series of books about:

FBA Product Sourcing

FBA Advance Traffic & Marketing Strategies

Amazon Wholesaling

Amazon Retail Arbitrage

Amazon Dropshipping

And many more books related to Amazon FBA.

If you want to make sure that you get a notification when these books go LIVE, just simply follow my Amazon author page.

(Click the follow button on that page to get instant updates from Amazon)

CPSIA information can be obtained
at www.ICGtesting.com
Printed in the USA
LVHW091515230322
714114LV00005B/228